The Inevitable Return of What We Do Not Love

a poem by

Julie Choffel

Finishing Line Press
Georgetown, Kentucky

The Inevitable Return of What We Do Not Love

a poem

Publisher: Leah Huete de Maines
Editor: Christen Kincaid
Cover Art: Omi Chang
Author Photo: Julie Choffel
Cover Design: Elizabeth Maines McCleavy

Order online: www.finishinglinepress.com
also available on amazon.com

Author inquiries and mail orders:
Finishing Line Press
PO Box 1626
Georgetown, Kentucky 40324
USA

here it comes again   the little gleam
the gem   forged under pressure   folded light
we stand in the cave   with wonder
going   who made this   going   not I
who's going to help me   make my own glittering nest
not I   said everyone   not I   then who's going to help me eat it
oh I will   we all can do that   we can eat everything   they said
we have   an insatiable appetite

I am scared   not of what could eat me   but what I could eat
going rabid over   what winds up inside of me
a tower of lives never lived
some prank   over the rainbow   I eat a heartbreak   I eat an itch
depending on the day I say
this is the sacrifice for knowing   this is the sacrifice for not

fortress like a rose bush   get a mattock   get a winch
destroyed   grows back   what's it trying   so hard for
never blooms   but in a parallel universe thrives   like   an accident
a clumsy stairwell   of roses
all over itself   can't get enough   of itself   that synthesis

when I go walking in shoes   often falling   you give me that look
like there I go again   falling in shoes

don't bother trying to quit bad habits unless   it's summer
have a pleasure   to make up for others   running can be a balm   if
you are already strong   otherwise just   pain on repeat   stop
stop   or you can just meditate   stop   stop
quit or don't quit

like dead love haunts   our dreams   some mixing of endings
I'm good with the future   no beef no quarrel   but is it good
with me   turning me over in my grave
like a map without   a legend   a codex   a trunk
a name like a list of other names

or another   version
I lowball the dealer   who looks at me eagle-eyed   and vain
a little gravity   steadies me finally   I retreat   how dare I think
it was even for sale

grace   come down now   if only
to make me feel   like color   like shape   were enough
like I'm not tripping on   the inevitable return
of what I do not   love
faceless   vulgar
I pin down   pulverize   forget

we don't know its real name   so we say sadness   nickname
shorthand   for closing eyes slowly   going deep
oh, hi   I found the other side
of my necklace   in the lake   I wake up   to the old friend

the wind comes in   won't settle
no one knows what for   this work   we just keep at it
stopping means death   to us   so the trick   is in   the pause
a possibility   of a next   or a gain at least in time   tiny ringing
in the ear   I'm nothing without   routine

an alphabet   a long   life
a myth for the ages   parades our success   myth being good
for feeling

a sheep in wolf's clothing   knows herself   better
the comparison is false   but   good for figuring
other things

god I just want to   connect
my stars   prick prick prick   my skin the line
but it's just a cover   stars say look look look   at the real dirt
it feels cool right   forget us   so far out of reach
focus   on your own job   focus

and dig   in don't   forget to look   at that   so many
ways to say I want   like using your eyes
the softening dirt   starting to give

so you see how   it circles   finding   a flaw
a host   in every sigh
nothing is ever done with us   each one of us   not
ever   over

the meal is something   I can appreciate
ground up   spiced and heated   tended just so   for my tongue
cheek   throat   body
how long would it take me   to tire of devour

you say   not long   I say   women are never
not hungry   even this talking   is not enough

the clematis extends   its arc   just long enough to reach
the sun   then stops   does nothing more
purple flowers are enough   silky seed heads are enough   living just
to continue   in each season   taking up only what it needs

does it include imagination   what is trying   anyway
I still can't say   if dance is separate moments   or an aggregate
but the body stays   in motion
I have barely begun   to move

the brain seeds the heart   which seeds the limbs
telling them   what's next   then back again in reverse
limbs heart brain   or   limbs brain heart   when something seizes
and you feel the echo   of adrenaline
in your exhaustion   a full sail

or a throughway to another   body   always making   even
when we don't want   to   someone else   we didn't mean to
and any   way you   interpret this   is what I mean too
like a new pathway   there I go
again   trying to liberate us   from what   we don't know

I hate that   it takes so long   to see
why we've done   what we've done   a castaway
remembers   the wreckage   more than the wreck
the material world   always winning   the consciousness

while action   shapes   us and then   disappears   from view
memory short   as a nerve

a girl   draws a maze   leading to the cure
if you do the right   dance
here goes   nothing   take   my hand   go hard on that air
for fast results   look for joy   on the face   like a path
to blue   or road   to the best kind of   nowhere

summer says forget   summer says   I have always
loved you this much   and nothing can keep me   from you

anyway time is a bummer   with its rasp   and cane
utter fuckery   but some days   it saves   and some days I
get ahead of it   over here   doggy

undulant earthen house   just tell me   or take me   as
if I could matter   on your tongue

so privacy   hits me hard   when I finally
get it   falling   through the spoken world
on my way down   my kids' questions   bomb me out   a target
with a caramel center

where is the language   for
me   where is the   floor
under the garbage   the sacred
place   within without
the blur   is real   across all wanting

what's left   of this zone anyway   the one we can sense now
depends upon   my access   to other zones
or say region
era   reach   arena
of the concrete   of the fluffy   fluffy concrete

along with   thoughts   maybe mine   maybe not
I am pushed to an edge   I give myself   the gift   of lipstick
on déjà vu   permission

there I go

what a mess   lurch of digital time   founding sense   of passing
depending on the day   remember when I took the
sculpture class   and it was awful   dull   only a rock inside my rock

only life inside this life   if I look at it that way
what's   not   to love

that objects have   a veneer   of permanence   in this
life   that they stay   even too long   on the earth
and our   strayed minds   can't find so much   as a cloud
to remind us

or   murmuration
looking like   pictures   sounding   like song
for a fraction
of the time it takes   to form   an idea of it   an identity
meanwhile a slow creep   behind the mind

why not try   to hold onto   that
the things are too dull and   long
the   not-things   not yet enough
though multiplying

how to stay   with it   the thing that plagues you   especially
when it's easy to look   away
from the plague   and the thing   has no teeth
just eyes that look back   and why can't   you sit   with curiosity
at very least   why is it born   as questions   little shields

the child rages   not with but at me   his originator
I see the pause in his eyes   calculating chances
for understanding   the beast in him   usually wins
for now

get this   we must pursue the single day
& holding space   for other days   like I have no patience
for bullshit   or bad manners
say please & thank you   to the future
even if it makes us cry   especially if it makes us   cry

a fissure in the box   lets in other air   a moth
a little mold   how novel   how new
what a chance   or what makes art   or what life
when art depends   on one's   reception   to the flux
the frequency   my son explains
is a pitch

I do better   when I write   but no guarantee   just better
than when I don't
sometimes there are friends here   sometimes
not   the plants   flourish   or die immediately   or slowly fade
then one day   the difference is clear

nothing ever really   ends   which could be impossible   to deal
with   an open frame   and a love of closing

think of specific things
a string   a bead   a bug crawling through
the system   oops   that's everything
do you know   how many feminist   poems
have moons   all the   prophesies the   same prophesy
of letters   made of pictures   turned over   in a rock tumbler

a temporary gloss   plus erosion   equals now
we must decide   if we care

about our later selves

can I even hold   one thing   in my mind   one safe   guard   we
almost never   we   require valence
and poppies

more and more   I see my suffering   from above
so it comes   from the side   at an angle   whatever
I may as well   lie down   and take it   flung awry   like so many
moonstones

made of problems   I go once more
towards
depending on depending on depending on   the earth
as in banking   as in betting   on snow
and birth control

just show me   already   how easy the boon
and fade   how to see

how to wear the pattern out   & about
to unbury the thought
from its outcome

the dirt   displaced
by my comfort   the comfort
replaced   by dirt

Julie Choffel is the author of the *The Hello Delay* (Fordham, 2012) and winner of the Poets Out Loud prize. Her poems can be found in *New American Writing, Posit, Orion, Barrow Street, Interim, Salamander,* and *the tiny,* among other places. Originally from Austin, Texas, she currently lives near Hartford and teaches at the University of Connecticut.